Transformation
In
Black and White

Transformation
In
Black and White

By

Lonzo Stanley
and
Dustin Frisbee

R. C. Linnell Publishing

Transformation in Black and White

Published by R. C. Linnell Publishing

Louisville, KY 40205

www.LinnellPublishing.com

Cover design: Dave Falkirk, Panoramic Creative Group

ISBN-13: 978-0-9961481-2-2

ISBN-10: 0-9961481-2-4

On the cover: Dustin Frisbee and Lonzo Stanley

About the Authors

Lonzo Stanley, a Muslim from the streets of Chicago, and Dustin Frisbee, a Christian from the mountains of Tennessee, cross boundaries set by religious radicals and break the code created by convicted killers and become the best of friends.

It all started in the F.C.I. Petersburg where the two served time together in an R-DAP (Residential Drug Abuse program). They realized that behind all their differences was a similar struggle. With a large dose of humility, the two shared in the victory of finding themselves.

When asked what they expect out of their stories, they answer simultaneously: "To be a part of someone's transformation." By reading this book, you will see their answer is genuine. They not only reveal the harsh truths that stand in the way of change; they expose the vulnerabilities in their own lives. Everyone who has read this book could not put it down. They were inspired and you will be also.

In this book you will find inspiration to take an honest look at yourself at the deepest level. In that moment you have the choice to forgive yourself and others. You can improve your life by finding the origins of your negative thinking patterns and replacing them with appropriate truths.

Give yourself a chance and let yourself live.

They did.

I dedicate this book to my loving mother, my "sister" Vickie, and my wonderful kids.

Lonzo Stanley

I dedicate this book to my loving mother and wonderful kids.

Dustin Frisbee

Contents

Introduction

The great poet William Wordsworth said "The child is father to the man." Inside the stories of these two men, both of whom grew up fatherless, you will find that this statement is true. You will also discover that their childhoods are not the final determinant of what they will become.

Every life has two stories: one you tell yourself and one that others tell about you. Both of these men have spent a good portion of their lives convincing themselves of the truth of one story, but an Omniscient Narrator looking from a distance would have seen quite another version.

For each of them, the path to reconcile those two stories was full of obstacles, self-deceit and catastrophic events. To survive at all took guts; to survive, overcome and to utterly reconfigure their whole beings from the ground up took nothing less than supernatural courage.

Courage. The root of the word is "cor," Latin for "heart." It literally means "having the heart" to do something. Knowing these men as I do, I can unequivocally say they demonstrate courage and have great hearts, too. I did not use the word "supernatural" casually either; they are both mighty men of faith, albeit two different ones.

To journey back deep into your own past to unearth the places where you got hurt, where you first lost your way, requires you to be unflinching. You cannot do it halfway. The light at the end of the proverbial tunnel most often appears dim and unreachable. It is one thing to attempt to find that for yourself. But these men have gone one step further; they want to help you see that

YOU, too, can take that journey successfully. If you're reading this, chances are you are already a survivor. Maybe you also felt forced to create a character and that "character" became you; it was what you projected.

Change is possible. Lonzo's and Dustin's stories prove that emphatically. Now that they have been transformed, they want you to join them on this journey. Read their stories and apply the truths of them where you can.

But remember, neither theirs nor your own journey is for the fainthearted; in fact, you need to approach it whole-heartedly. That means you can't stop with reading this or even with being inspired by it. You need to do what it takes, to dig deep and consult your own Omniscient Narrator as to what His plan is for you. At minimum, my advice is to pass this book on to another and to push forward the work these brave men have started.

Reconcile your two stories. Rewrite the ending. Father your child that wasn't loved enough. Move forward with courage. Let the lion that has roared inside you lay down beside the lamb of peace.

Professor Ricks

Part I

WE LOST OURSELVES

Chapter 1
I Lost Myself
Lonzo

Mom was addicted to crack. That meant we struggled just to survive. We did not have much money to begin with, and whatever blessings fell upon us turned to ash. They became the source of her next fix.

I love Mom so much. I just wanted her to be happy. I remember times when she would be the best mom in the world. Because we didn't have much, we lived in the basement of an apartment building. I knew why she went into the bathroom there. It didn't even bother me that much, because I just wanted to see her happy.

And when she came out, she WAS happy. This made me okay with what she was doing. It was just as elating for me because I was comforted by her joy. When she was fiending for a fix she would be angry. It would be obvious something was more important than us. When she started jonesing, I could see it. I wanted my Momma sober. I wanted her free of the obvious distress she was in.

I woke up one morning and she was crying. She was saying how I needed to get out and find a job to help pay the bills. The lights were off and she was too far into her addiction to find work outside the home.

She ran an extension cord from the neighbor's house with a power strip attached to it. We plugged lamps, hot pots, and the TV into it. I enjoyed those moments because we would get blankets, hug and enjoy each other's comfort. Mom was not focused so much on the crack in those moments and I was able to soak in her love.

I woke up early one Friday morning. I carried the lamp to the bathroom mirror and got myself together, I was feeling optimistic. I believed I could do what the crack couldn't do for my mother. I would get a job and turn the lights on. I was thirteen.

I started practicing what I would say to the store owners in the mirror: "Do y'all need any help? I will stack boxes, sweep the parking lot, take out the trash. Is there anything I can do to earn some money?"

I was determined to get a job. I was practicing my best smile. And when I left the apartment I did not wake mom. I turned off the lamp, kissed her on the cheek and started my journey full of hope. On the West Side of Chicago there were like a hundred shopping stores on Madison Street. And that's where I was headed to get my first job.

On the way to the stores my spirits were high. I remember visualizing myself working for the Pakistani owners. I had actual conversations with them in my mind. Their sing-song voices answered me back in their foreign accents. They would encourage me, praise me for my good work, and I would give them my best smile. They would pay me. I would carry the money to my mom and she would feel like she did when she'd just come out of the bathroom. I could make mom happy like she made me happy when she covered me up when I was sick and made me soup.

It was going to be okay because I was smart. The first store I went to, the cashier could not understand me. I had to keep repeating myself and then he said, "No." He did not need any help. I was still optimistic and I practiced out loud all the way to the next store.

I was determined to get a job. I walked in the next store and a lady was standing directly in front of me. It looked perfect! She looked me straight in the eye and smiled as I opened the door. I gave her my best, trying to sell myself as a hard worker. She patted me on the shoulder and said that the owner would be in later that evening if I wanted to come back and ask him. She gave me a piece of gum and I left to make my way to the next store.

I was full of energy and everything seemed perfect. I knew today was going to be the best day of my life. I was going to do for my mom what she could not do for herself, because I was a man.

I was smart, I was determined, and I got this drive from my mom. I'd seen her go through so much and never quit until she got what she set out to get. I was going to get this job.

Much later, my sneakers slapped the pavement and each step seemed to rub new blisters. I must have gone to a hundred plus stores. It was getting near dark and I was approaching the last store within walking distance. I wiped my mouth with the underside of my sleeve, stood up a little bit straighter and walked in.

The man inside looked at me like I was his enemy. I gave him my best smile and poured out my lines with passion. He said that he did not need help, that I was just a kid and should be in school somewhere. I dropped my head and walked out the door, but before I could step out he hollered, "KID!" I turned around and he also threw me a piece of bubble gum.

The daylight had bled away and streetlights bathed the concrete beneath me. My earlier optimism had faded with the light, but somewhere, deep inside, I knew I could still do this. I was discouraged, but still on course. I was more than a "kid." I was a bright young man and would prove myself. I would not give up. My mom didn't give up and I wouldn't either.

Pounding the pavement home, I remember coming across a sound that was familiar but to which I'd never paid full attention before: voices chanting, "Rocks, blows, park, rocks, blows, park." I looked over and saw other young men, my age, in high spirits quoting this Chicago mantra: "Rocks, blows, park." It seemed productive. These guys were active. They were doing something, accomplishing something. The words themselves meant, I learned, that they had "rocks" to sell, and "blow," and you had to park to get them.

I made it back home and went right to Mom's room. She was gone. I was exhausted, but my hunger pains forbade me to sleep. I got up and made a ketchup sandwich. I went to sleep. When I woke up the next morning, the first thing I heard in my mind was "you're just a kid." It was in that foreign accent that was so hard to understand and now, somehow, so sinister. But now it was clear in my mind. I closed my eyes again and saw the store owner throw me a piece of gum. I was "just a kid." He did not believe in me. He did not believe I could help him. He thought I was just a kid and he disrespected me with his bubble gum. I began to hate those stores and what they represented. I even stopped liking bubble gum.

The women in my family were accomplished thieves. I never could steal like my mom and sisters. I would always freeze up. They would call me "pussy," "coward," and they said I lacked courage. The store owners had called me "kid" and the grownups pegged me as a "pussy and a coward."

They did not realize who they were talking to. I did not need their jobs, or stolen goods. I ate my favorite -- a bread and syrup sandwich -- and when I stepped out of the house I heard again "Rocks, blows, park."

A.J. was posted up out front with Ray. They owned the block I lived on. What got my attention was Lil Tony standing with them. He was the same age as me. I had beat him up in school when he had mouthed at me. I knew I was not a pussy because I had beat this dude up. And now he was running with A.J. and Ray? Wearing a chain and a new outfit? Sweet...

I walked up mugging Tony, daring him to return my glare, anxious for Round Two. I asked A.J. with the same passion I had asked the stores for something to do. He did not turn me down. He sensed my courage from the way I had mugged Tony. He believed in me and proved it. He pulled me off to the side and put me up on game: I was to sit at the end of the alley and watch for the police. I was security. It was my job to let the pack man know if the police were coming. This paid sixty dollars a day. Twelve hour shifts that started and ended at twelve. If I slipped and did not see the police, my pay would be docked.

I knew I was a man. A.J. put thirty dollars in my pocket before I got started and in that moment I found my place. It was from these guys that I would learn who I was. I did not value the opinions of anyone else, so I ignored them. Everyone else was confused about who I was. A.J. and Ray knew I was a man and I used their words and example to form my own unique identity and independence.

I was now able to help take care of my family. I bought my oldest sister, Terry, Italian Beefs, and my little sister, Pam, some "Flamin' Hot" chips. Mom and my middle sister, Candy, liked money, so I gave them cash.

I was not a "pussy." I was not a "kid." I was THE MAN and I proved it. These people did not know who I was. Nobody understood me for real, but I would get my respect and acknowledgement from the ones who believed in me. From the ones who gave me a chance.

My family began to expect something from me. My responsibility increased, but my pay was still sixty dollars a day. I had to advance in my job, so I went from security to pack man. My pay rose from sixty dollars a day to one hundred.

I began to understand why A.J. was so hard on people. My mom and sisters quit appreciating my favors and started demanding them. I had to change my game up. Mom was trying to treat me like a kid when I would not give her what she wanted. I had to start being the boss. She could not do what I could and I knew it. I was a man and people were going to respect me like one.

Early one morning, I was working the pack in the alley when Man-Man walked up and asked me where the pack was. He was known throughout the hood for robbing people. He had no fear. Everyone hated to see him coming. He was a dude just waiting on someone to kill him. He smacked me in my face. I was picking myself up off the ground when he lifted his shirt, showing me his thumper. I gave him my pack. I went and found the overseer who distributes the packs to me and told him I'd been robbed. He asked who it was and when I told him, he said okay and gave me another pack. It was like nothing had happened. They'd expected this. They must've thought I was just a kid too.

Two weeks later, A.J. and Ray picked me up and started pressing me to handle my business. They said they didn't need any kids out there. That I was gonna put work in. I was gonna prove myself. They told me where Man-Man was as they handed me the thumper across the car seat. They dropped me off just up the block from his location, but the walk felt like an eternity. Then when I saw him I wished I had another eternity between us. I closed my eyes and did what I was supposed to do and became a celebrity overnight.

I lost myself to the streets that night. A.J., Ray and anybody who was somebody in the street praised me. I had done their dirty work. I did what they were scared to do and they called me "crazy." They looked up to me and I enjoyed my new status. I wasn't just a kid. I was a MAN!

Lonzo's Explanation

My mother, she's my baby. Even in her addiction she was the queen of queens in my eyes. As a kid I knew something wasn't right, but with a mother like mine, it didn't feel like nothing was wrong either. I was thirteen years old when my mother was complaining about the lights and how I needed to get out and find a job to help around the house. I can't explain the enthusiasm I had going on to find that dream job of mine. Not getting that job done something to me that I suppressed and put some false pride on top of by thinking up some good-for-me-at-the-time thoughts. But they were ultimately negative things I achieved which gave me the strength and courage to approach A.J.. This mold that I went into took me on a road to losing my true self.

I started out to help my mother and my siblings. My intentions were pure and innocent. I just wanted to help stop the suffering of my family and when the positive world didn't accept me and that negative, illusion world did, my intentions were still the same. They just weren't so pure and innocent now.

I did what I intended to do. I helped take care of my family. I pitched in around the house. I was able to give my mother money and my older sisters and younger sister whatever they asked me for. That was my dream in life! I was living my dream life, so I couldn't even see the wrong I was doing in the streets. And that's what that illusion world does to us. It makes wrong feel so right when you're putting a smile on your loved ones faces, and that, in itself, stops you from seeing what you are doing to other people and their loved ones.

Jumping into that illusion world took me on a thirteen year journey of organized criminal activities that got me arrest after arrest and into shootout after shootout. The last war I was in on the Chicago streets was too much for me. It was with some heavy hitters in the same organization I was in. They were about to run into my mother's house one day and, all praise to God, they didn't. I saw they weren't playing fair, so I called one of the guys and told him that they could have all that street stuff, just keep my family out of it. I packed up my work (drugs) and headed to the place where my children's grandmother lived. That's how I ended up in Madison, Wisconsin. I wasn't down there a whole year, doing and acting the same way I had been on Chicago's streets, and in Wisconsin, that is a no-no. The Feds indicted me in 2003.

Chapter 2
Who Am I?
Dustin

"Son...son...wake up."

Minutes pass.

"Get up sweetie, let's go home."

"No, mom, I'm going to stay here."

"No, son, come on, it's late."

"What time is it?"

"It's one o'clock."

"Why do you always come wake me up so late?"

"Because I love you, son, and I do not want you staying away from me when I'm not at work."

More minutes pass.

"Come on, let's go."

Still more minutes pass.

"I already put your bicycle in the trunk."

Mom has been working two jobs for as long as I can remember. I was getting too big to carry to the car. She had to wake me up when she got off work. The next morning always came early. Mom was tired and when I did not get up immediately she got a bit angry.

"Get up, son."

And finally:

"GET YOUR BUTT UP; I'm not going to keep telling you!"

I still stayed in bed until the very last minute. Then I jumped up and put on the pants mom had bought me the week before when Mr. Seymour had sent me home with a note for dress code failure. I kissed Mom goodbye, jumped on my bicycle and raced to the bus stop. I was riding a wheelie coming out of the driveway when my pants leg got caught in the sprocket. They ripped about six inches up the side. And I had no time to be going back home to change. I tucked them in my sock and jumped back on my bike, trying to make the bus.

When I got to school I stood in line as we made our way through the front doors. Each morning I noticed everyone's L.L. Bean backpacks, but this particular morning Ben Preston's stood out to me, maybe because I had heard Ms. Price speak to his dad, Mr. Preston, on her way in. When she said his name, I happened to be reading Ben's on his backpack at the same time, noticing the carefully stitched letters. I was self-conscious that I did not have an L.L. Bean backpack. For that matter, I did not even have my dad's last name.

When I got to the door, Mr. Seymour pulled me to the side and asked me what was wrong with my pants. I pulled them out of my sock and they fell over my shoe like bell bottoms. I told him I would safety pin them, but he advised me that I could not stay, that is was a violation of dress code.

In the office, I tried calling mom, but did not get an answer. I paged her on her beeper and was waiting on her call back when she came bouncing through the front door. She did not waste any time.

"What is it now?" she demanded from the secretary, with her hand on her hip.

"Ms. Frisbee, I know you are upset, but we have told you on several occasions everyone here is required to follow the dress code."

"Y'all should be dammed ashamed of y'all's self, keeping my boy from getting an education because he does not wear what y'all want him to wear. I'm sick of this school and all y'all hypocrites who work here. I'm signing him out today."

Mom signed me out of school and drove me to work with her. At work she turned into the nicest lady I'd ever met. I enjoyed watching her stand in front of the class and teach sign language. The morning went by pretty fast. By the time three o'clock rolled around I was worn out, but mom was just halfway through her day.

She had another job at a local gas station where she worked until midnight. A couple hours after we got to the gas station, mom called Grandma to pick me up. Grandma is deaf and does not hear the phone a lot of times. Mom called Kenny, who lived next door in a camper, and he said he would come get me but needed gas money. When he got there, Mom gave him twenty dollars and told him to take me straight to Grandma's.

Kenny was addicted to crack cocaine. We went downtown to St. Elmo and met a guy on the side of the road named Gator. Gator sold Kenny a little pebble for

17

twenty dollars and we pulled into a car wash up the street. Kenny asked me if I wanted to try it. I asked him what it would do to me.

He replied, "It's just going to make your lips sweat."

I wondered why in the hell would you pay twenty dollars to make your lips sweat. But what the hell, Ill try it.

Out loud, I answered "Yeah, I guess."

He held the pipe and lit it for me, but my lips did not sweat. I did not feel anything, but I do know he did. When he hit it, he started being really weird. He was looking all around and kept asking me if I heard something. I was kind of scared because he made me think something was going to happen. But after a minute he calmed down and we finally started the drive to Grandma's. I smoked cigarettes all the way there, thinking I was the coolest thing in the world.

When I got to Grandma's, I thought about all that had happened that day. I realized I was somehow smarter then Kenny but less fortunate than Ben.

I waited for mom to get home. When she pulled up, she did not have to wake me up. I hugged her neck as soon as she walked through the door. She broke down and cried, hugging me tighter.

What's wrong, Mom?

"Nothing, I just love you, son."

"I know you do, Mom, it's going to be okay."

"What happened to your pants?"

I told her and she shook her head.

"Every pair of shoes you get, you ruin on that bicycle and now it's your pants. Momma can't afford to keep buying you clothes, son. There is not enough hours in the day as it is."

"I know, Mom, but if I could go to Dunlap schools, it would not matter. I could wear the jeans Uncle Matt gave me."

"It looks like you're gonna have to, because we are moving. I can't afford this house by myself and there is a trailer for rent across the county line."

YAAYYY!!! I was happy. All my friends lived across the county line. And I could wear whatever I wanted to school.

My friend John Levi lived up the street. I always stayed at John's because his mom let us smoke weed. His family had a push mower and a Weed Eater. We knocked on every door in walking distance, soliciting yards to cut and trim. We had a good week about halfway through the summer. Then his older brother, Drew, peeped our hustle. He invited us to go with him and my Uncle Matt. We were excited to hang out with the older guys. We jumped straight in the car with them.

We pulled out of the driveway and met Brent at the circle down the street where everyone parked. Drew and Brent cleverly tricked John and me out of our money. We were standing there with steam coming out our ears when Maria pulled up. She asked us what was wrong and we told her. We knew she was the best weed dealer in town, but everyone had always made us wait in the car when we went to her house to deal. She gave us an ounce on credit and her beeper number too.

19

We enjoyed our walk back home.

We broke that ounce down, crushing seeds and cutting up stems. We rolled seventy joints for three dollars each. When Drew came in he was surprised to find us in high spirits. By then we were hip to him and his cowardly ways. We knew he was bigger and stronger but not smarter. He bought a three dollar joint from us and we laughed when a seed popped in his face, knowing we had already earned the money once. We sold every last joint within two days. Drew's girlfriend Debbie gave us a ride to re-up.

I remember feeling so grown up at eleven years old while rolling a joint to smoke with her on the way back.

<hr>

The next few years flew by in a drug-fueled haze.

By the time I was thirteen, I was addicted to cocaine.

I would sell weed to support my habit. I quit school when I was fifteen. I went to Juvenile for possession of marijuana at seventeen. And Katie had my baby girl Madison right before my nineteenth birthday. If nothing else had already, her birth should have been the game-changer for me.

I had always told myself that I would never abandon my kid as my dad had abandoned me. I tried to stop using. I would look into my daughter's pretty blue eyes and make a conscious effort to stop thinking about drugs but the desire to use would always win.

I went to Grandpa's for ten days to help him build a barn. My intentions were to get my system clean so I would hopefully have the willpower to maintain sobriety. When we finished, I had him drop me off at the gas station close to my house. I'd been drinking to help my come-down. Grandpa told me to be good; I told him I would and that I was meeting a girl. I was actually waiting on my dope man, a homeboy I had called ahead of time.

I was anticipating my next high when a gang member I had fought with months prior pulled up. I approached his car and he shot me twice in the torso, knocking me to the ground.

I almost died. I remember being in the hospital with a ten percent chance to live. I could hear everyone around me talk, worry, and panic. I was unable to move. I couldn't even open my eyelids or nod my head.

I was in-patient for several days. It was a horrible experience, but still not enough to change my lifestyle. Neither juvenile arrest, my daughter's birth, nor getting shot and nearly dying had been enough!

Six months later, I was in another shooting. I fired a round through my roof when two guys tried to rob me. And one of them, in turn, shot through my front door seventeen times. When the cops came, they found twelve grams of cocaine. This time the judge sentenced me to five years.

I spent time with my Dad for the first time while in the county jail where I was held over waiting to be sent to state prison. He helped me get ready for prison life. We smuggled tobacco and manipulated my mom.

When I arrived at Brushy Mountain State Penitentiary my first celly was president of the Aryan nation and serving a life sentence for murder. He was very influential, but also addicted to heroin. I soon traded my cocaine habit for a heroin addiction. This new drug was more convenient and fitting within the prison. Whatever human decency I had left evaporated. I left prison four years and seven months later. I was a monster at twenty-six years old.

Dustin's Explanation

The school that had sent me home for a dress code violation is the best school in my area for academics. When I left that school, I left with a resentment toward "rich" people. I was upset that I was not given a chance to show that I could improve.

I chose on that day a path that I could excel on. A path that accepted me. I became very clever, very fast in the world in which I did not belong. My mother tried everything she could, but being a woman, and working the way she had to support us, she could not be there or be the role model I needed.

The people I looked up to had drugs and drinking as a big part of their lives. I can look back now and see good in everyone who negatively influenced me. I still don't understand why I saw good in what would ultimately destroy my life.

Your Transformation Story
How did you lose yourself?

At the end of each section there will be questions to help you think about your situation and face the facts that got you where you are. Be honest. Write it all down, the good and the bad. Be as specific as you can.

Don't worry about grammar or punctuation or anything besides getting your story on paper. It's not enough to think about it. Your story must be written. You can do it in small segments as your mind starts thinking about it. Write down the event you're thinking of and put it away for a couple of days. Then come back and read it. Did you remember more? Write that down also.

Keep adding to your story until it feels complete. You'll know when that happens. You will read all your notes and you will get a feeling of satisfaction, of completeness, of accomplishment. It may take days, weeks or even months until it feels right. Keep going until you get that feeling. Then you are ready to go on to the next section.

We've given you some questions to get you started. Don't limit yourself to just these questions. Expand your story as necessary.

> ➤ How did you lose yourself?
> ➤ Where did your road to destruction begin?
> ➤ Who influenced you?
> ➤ How old were you when it started?
> ➤ What were the determining factors in the decisions you made?

> Did anyone try to help? Why didn't you take their help?

> How would you describe yourself? How would others describe you?

> Where did it take you?

Write it down.

Part II

WHO WE BECAME

Chapter 3
I'm in Character
Lonzo

It was late June 2003. I stepped out of the Madison City deputy's car and walked into the Wisconsin Federal Courthouse.

I will never forget that day. It was like I was attending my own funeral. The prosecutor began to read my eulogy: "Lonzo J. Stanley has been a menace to society. If it was up to me he would spend the rest of his life in prison. He's a member of a notorious Chicago street gang called the 'New Breed, Black Gangsters,' a drug dealer and three time convicted felon. He has committed many crimes at many levels and absolutely refuses to cooperate with law enforcement. He does not show remorse nor does he appear to be affected by the guidelines of his current charge."

What made the prosecutor so mad actually relieved my resentment and I held my head high, proud of my strength. "The United States of America versus Lonzo J. Stanley" is what my indictment read, but I didn't break.

Smile.

But then I heard my family behind me begin to cry. I saw tears roll down their cheeks, but I was too far in my criminal lifestyle to crumble. I sincerely apologized for hurting them, for putting them through this, and to society for everything I had done that harmed or affected someone in a negative way. I did this as sincerely as I could, but when I got to my breaking point I cut my emotions off.

When the judge said "Two hundred months," I did not allow his words to penetrate. I heard him but I was not ready to close my casket's lid. I told myself and my family I was okay and not to cry.

When I got back to the county jail I went to my bunk and lay down. The judge's words: "Two hundred months" were echoing in my head. I was calculating, trying to figure out how many years I would be buried and the number was echoing louder and louder inside my head.

Then a real voice came through the vent:

"Zo? Zo? Zo?"

I jumped out of my bed and stepped up on the toilet to listen. "Yeah," I answered.

"What them crackers give you?"

"Ah, just a little seventeen years!"

"SEVENTEEN YEARS?" he screamed.

I laughed like it was nothing and this helped me feel better. It felt good that I was being strong and I became stronger by other people feeling my pain. For the first time, someone was acknowledging what I was going through.

I had been covering up what I did not understand within me for so long. I had become good at enduring what was breaking everyone else down. This gave me a sense of accomplishment, but the cold hard truth was that I was lying in my casket and would be staying there for "SEVENTEEN YEARS". Still I refused to be a victim. At least the lid was still open and I was not yet in the ground.

"Mr. Stanley." the officer called.

"Yeah," I answered.

"Pack up, you're going to R and D (Receiving and Departures.)"

I looked around. My cell was already empty - a seven by nine room of whitewashed concrete I'd called home for ten months.

"I'm ready."

I cuffed up and walked the short distance to intake. The guard shackled my feet and locked my handcuffs to a belly chain. Then he escorted me to a bus headed to McKean, Pennsylvania, FCI McKean, a medium security Prison for federal inmates.

I remember sitting on the bus by the window. My mind was focused on my new life. I was anxious to get some commissary, hygiene, a shower, and to have a bunk to lay my head down on at night. I know I did not have much to look forward to, but coming from a county jail with the bare minimum necessities, the small things mean a whole lot.

Looking out the bus window in a daydream, I saw something that caught my eye and took me straight back to the past. I don't know if it was the same woman, but she looked exactly like the lady who gave me bubble gum at that second store all those years ago. Most cars were passing by our bus, but this woman stayed right beside my window. I could see her, but she couldn't see me through the mirror-tinted windows that make us prisoners invisible during transfers.

Her presence took me back to the Chicago streets, to a day and time when I had an honest ambition. I imagined where I would be today if she'd given me that job instead of a piece of bubble gum. I was making mental notes of possibilities, comparing starting points and destinations, where they led:

Parking lot sweeper versus watchman.

Cashier versus packman.

My own store versus my own block.

The "what ifs" were depressing me.

"Don't start crying now," a guy hollered three seats behind me. I thought to myself, "How did he read my thoughts?" I shut my feelings off and turned with conviction to confront him. He was chastising a young white kid for crying.

When I turned back around the woman in the car was speeding off like she somehow knew that I had been drawn back into reality.

Seventeen years.

When I stepped off the bus into this new world, FCI McKean, it was like they had dropped off a seasoned vet at training school. I had already been through and done so much. What I'd been doing at thirteen, these dudes were just learning.

I had reason to be proud. In my world, I had been at the top.

I was immediately given the shot caller position for the "Black Gangsters." That meant I said who did what and when; I had the respect and responsibility equivalent of a Mafia Don in the prison world. I also got a job as a grade one in the plumbing shop, which gave me access to all the tools.

I was making stuff happen and everybody knew it. For the most part, my fellow Gangstas liked it. They would watch and wonder how in the world I was so bold with it. I would be thinking to myself, "How in the world can they be so broken and weak?"

It was not long before excitement turned into envy and the counselor called me into her office.

"Mr. Stanley, I have received three notes on you this week. They say you are making wine, selling drugs and tobacco. This is your warning. You keep it up, I am going to ship you."

I blew her off and continued to do what I did without reservation. I had my hands on a little bit of everything, living the penitentiary life to the fullest. About five write-ups or incident reports later, I was sent to the SHU (Special Housing Unit). I was being held there until they could get me to a higher security prison.

I was locked down twenty-three hours a day, seven days a week. This may sound crazy, but when they told me I was going to Terre Haute, Indiana, the SHU was suddenly not so bad. I knew this game was getting ready to change. I was going to the United States Penitentiary, a place for America's worst criminals - Terre Haute in particular- it was a death row joint.

I turned my workout up. Instead of working out once a day, I started going twice a day. I also began to strategically seek information from other dudes about what to expect at this new spot I was going to. I tried to listen for clues without asking questions.

I remembered the way I used the trainees' questions against them, turning their concern into weakness and treating them accordingly.

When I was in intake at Terre Haute I overheard people there talking. The prison was on lockdown because someone had just got killed. They were saying this nonchalantly like it was a normal everyday event. It just so happened that this time it was in the block I was being placed in.

We stayed on lockdown a few more days and when we came off, the place was everything I had expected and then some. And I don't mean in a positive way. These dudes were some real gangstas. They were not faking. My homeboys from the city ran down on me, found out who I was and confirmed it, and started treating me accordingly.

They had a welcome bag for me, filled with food, stamps, clothes, wine, etc. After I showed them my paperwork, I got the yard - meaning the shot caller position for the organization. I was in, and man, this opened up doors for me.

I had to be on my toes now. The game-playing was over; it was life or death in this joint. My homeboys did their best and I had an attitude like I was invincible. It did not matter where they put me. I was gonna excel. There was nothing anyone could do to stop it. I said to myself, "As long as this casket lid is open, this mind is gonna be spinning off ideas and casting off its authority."

Then one day I was on the top tier watching the homeboys make a move on one of our own. He was actually my buddy, and they were trying to entrap him into a violation. I thought, "It doesn't have to go that way." But it was always this way in the joint. You had to worry about your homeboys more than the white supremacists. I realized in that moment that I was gonna have to close the casket lid to the world I knew.

I was gonna have to enter a dark lonely place and refuse to peek out for the slightest comfort. I had to die to everything I had ever known. I had to give up everything that was beneficial to me. I had to forsake my safety and social position for the hope of the life that was so far away you needed a telescope to see it.

I do not know how or why I saw it when I did, but I decided it was worth becoming a nobody. Now it is one thing to lose all recognition in hopes of a better way, but to lose recognition along with security of your livelihood is to be buried alive. This place, this state of mind I entered became so dark, so lonely that I felt as if I could not go on. The environment I was in - The United States Penitentiary - was too cold for crying.

I was surrounded but so alone. I had stepped down from my position, out of my peer group and this felt like I'd closed the lid of my casket.

My big homies used to make comments and tempt me back into their world.

"Come on, Zo, you know such and such is fixin' to hit."

"Come on, boy, you fakin'."

"Come hit this wine."

"Come on boy, whadya do, turn into a square?"

I would be sitting on the top tier by myself, consternated between good and evil when these dudes came with their confident comments. The anxiety I experienced felt as if clumps of clay were hitting my casket lid already. The dirt was coming faster and faster until I couldn't take it anymore. The old world was pouring in on me.

If I did not push the lid open, accept their invitations back into the world that was familiar to me, I would be forever forgotten. I would be an official nobody. The pressure was too much to bear alone. My body began to shake. Doubt dominated my mind. I did not have to keep fighting this battle. I could push the lid open. I could take their invitations. I could do what I'd been doing all my life. And DAMN! Here he comes......

Lonzo's Explanation

In the courtroom I had felt big, strong and proud of myself. But I couldn't understand what I was so proud and strong about. When the dude called me in the vent and reminded me of how much of a real dude I was for standing strong against the federal government and taking them two hundred months like a soldier, that gave me the answer I needed. At that moment in that cell, couldn't nobody tell me or convince me that that was false pride and false strength I was operating on.

When I thought about my family's faces in the courtroom I got weak so I had to think about my criminal activities and how I hold my own weight to make me strong. I hated to feel weak and on that bus ride to McKean, that's what I felt. I thought about beliefs that made me strong, so when I hit the yard, I did everything a young uneducated twenty-six year old Chicago street gang member would do. They didn't know how to deal with me in Pennsylvania, so they sent me up my way to Terre Haute, Indiana, which changed my life forever.

Entering into Terre Haute, I had a more humble state of mind because I know I was dealing with the same caliber of dudes that I grew up with, so I didn't go right in getting into all that wild stuff because I know that type of behavior would get me killed there. But as I got settled in and got positioned to how I wanted to be and five years into that jungle world, it just hit me: "Man, you're tripping. Five years went by and you don't have nothing, you don't know nothing, you can't even read the letter your son just wrote you a week ago. No GED, no nothing! You been drunk the whole five years. You been here five years stuck at the poker table day in and day out, catching write-ups for knives, fights, wine and everything else. You is a fool; you got an out date, you got a second chance to try to get it right. These guys don't care if they don't wake up in the morning. Lonzo, you can't keep living in that illusional world!"

It came to me just like that. And shortly after that I started going to my GED class. I stopped caring what people would think about me not knowing how to read or write.

There were two great tutors in the class I was in, Twelve and Shocker. I owe a lot to those two individuals. They found out that I couldn't read and it was like they put everything else to the side. I hated them at times. I would be walking out on the yard with a group of my guys and they would pull me over and tell me to spell "house" or something. Man, I would be mad as hell and tell them to go somewhere, but they were real stand-up men and they didn't let me leave without spelling the word they asked me to spell. I love them for their dedication. But as I was coming to learn new things and also becoming aware of what was really going on around me, I was starting to become uncool.

I was starting to become "fake" as they called me. It seemed like the guys started to feel like I was betraying them or leaving them hanging. And by me not drinking or playing poker, nor making moves, I was starting to feel alone. This new world was a lonely place. I started questioning myself: "Am I doing the right thing?" It was starting to feel NOT so right. It wasn't real excitement over here and the guys I loved, admired and some I looked up to were living in what I know now is an illusional world. I asked myself "Do you think you still have street cred? Do they still see me as a

Gangsta? Do they see me as a square? How did I go from the main attraction to a nobody?"

And one day, as I was thinking all this, one of the realest gangstas I knew when I was in that world walked up to me.

"DAMN!"

Chapter 4
This is Not Me
Dustin

I was on my back porch drinking Budweiser, crying tears of self-pity, flipping a broken-tipped pocket knife open and closing it back on my leg. I was sick of myself. I did not do the things I wanted to do, but the things I did not want to do.

I was a slave to heroin.

I had been calling rehabs all morning. With no money nor insurance, I had no luck. Fueled by the need for another fix and almost equally by the wish for sobriety, I developed a plan to rob all my drug dealers. This plan would meet both of my needs: I could get a fix and at the same time close off the means of getting a future fix.

This thinking led me into another near death experience and earned me a first degree attempted murder charge. I robbed them, went home and passed out. When I was up again, a rehab called and said they had a bed available for me for free. The girl I was with said she would go with me and we decided to get high together first. Two days later, I went to jail in a drug-induced coma.

I woke up in a cold shower cell trying to remember what exactly I did or did not do. Finally, I moved into a state of acceptance: at least I could get sober now.

I had been in jail for a couple of months when my celly received a settlement. He made both our bonds and while I was out on bond I met Lauren. She already had two kids. We all moved into an apartment together. I started experiencing life as a somewhat responsible adult. It felt good to be able to pay bills (though I did that with both legally and illegally obtained money), and to take the kids to school and to cook out on the grill. I had never done these things before; I had never done anything except what the drugs wanted me to do.

While I was out on the state charges, the feds indicted me on felony possession of a firearm. Then the U.S. Marshals started kicking down doors looking for me. I went into panic mode. I could feel myself slipping from rationality. I had to make a choice: jail or freedom. It would not be long before they found out where I lived.

I could rob a bank and go on the run - my irrational thoughts were telling me - or I could turn myself in.

Lauren and I took the kids to a babysitter and drove out of town to buy a little more time. We slept at a friend's house that night, holding each other tight. She loved me so much that night. She encouraged me to stay with her. I felt she would do anything in the world to help me and when I told her I was going to turn myself in, she cried hysterically. She hugged me so tight and I embraced her back, knowing that I had to go and go soon before I changed my mind. This was the hardest decision I'd ever had to make, but I was an adult now and I had to take control of my own life somehow.

I drove straight to the county jail and walked through the front doors. This time was going to be different from the past; I was going to get an education and, most importantly, I was going to come out a better man, the man I knew in my heart that I could be.

I had three days until court and I drove my celly crazy. He said I was "buggin' out." I had papers scattered all over the room: on the desk, floor, and taped to the wall. I had a pencil behind each of my ears and one in my hand. I was trying to summarize my life story up in one speech for my sentencing statement. I believed that if the judge knew exactly who I was behind the drugs, I would get exactly what I deserved and come out of lockup as Dustin 2.0, new and improved. Every two or three minutes I would tap my celly on the shoulder and tell him to listen. I then would read him a couple of lines, such as: "I have been under the influence of drugs and alcohol in every crime I have ever committed."

I would do this while pacing back and forth in the cell. Three steps, turn around, three steps, turn around, three steps and turn around. Every so often I would bend down, scratch some lines out, add a few more and then ask my celly to listen: "I stand here today a man who has rebelled against all authority. I chose to live a life of crime and to use drugs to manipulate myself and everyone around me."

I continued this process until about 2:00 a.m. I finally got my statement summarized. Then I began to commit it to memory. When my family came to visit that weekend, I was able to recite it for them word for word. I had put everything I had into that speech, so when Mom told me I sounded "like a robot," I got a little upset. I wanted it to be moving, to stir the judge's compassion.

I went to court the next day. The judge asked me if I had anything to say. I began speaking, but before I got halfway through I was crying. Every word of it was true and it was so hard actually admitting these things, even though eliciting sympathy had been my motivation. The court reporter teared up. Even my lawyer was speechless. The judge said, "One of three things will happen to you: one, you will spend the rest of your life in prison; two, you will be killed; three, you will be rehabilitated."

Then he sentenced me to ninety months in prison. I told my family that this time it was going to be like college for me. I was going to get myself together. Educate myself. Then, when I was leaving the county jail, I found out I was having a son by a girl I hardly knew.

When I arrived at U.S.P. McCreary I was determined to do these things. I had never considered myself a person who is easily influenced but I did not understand the politics of federal penitentiaries. There were some things my dad could not have prepared me for. When I walked through the unit doors, it was already past 9:00 p.m. and the unit was locked down for the night. The officer on duty told me what cell to go to, but an inmate stopped me before I could get there by tapping on his cell window. When I walked up to his door, curious, he said, "Don't go in the cell with a nigger."

I went on to my cell. Early the next morning, this same guy woke me up. He had a couple of guys with him. I had plenty of reason to be upset, but common sense told me to be humble. They escorted me down to a cell where a little old man was sitting on the back wall under the eerie glow of a book light.

This man began to run down the rules to me:

Whites are always to stick together

You cannot go to chow by yourself.

You cannot talk to an officer, counselor, or case manager without someone else with you.

At all times, you must have your boots on.

You have to show your paperwork within thirty days (to prove you're not a sex offender or snitch) and when you get cleared, we will give you one of these. He nodded towards a knife on the desk behind him.

Then he began to explain that I would have to "put in work:" physically hurt someone who was breaking one of the rules he had just explained to me.

I replied, "Look, I respect everything you said because it doesn't look like I have much of a choice, but I'm not going to be your crash dummy. I'm trying to get an education and stay out of trouble."

Everyone in the room laughed.

"Don't worry," he finally said, "I will be right there with you. We will do it together." He spoke calmly. He had a cold tone to his voice that chilled me and made me worry about catching an additional charge. At least if I was the one "putting in the work," I thought I could judge how far to go with it. This old man talked of

45

these things like they were recreation, a sporting activity.

Prison was not going to turn out like I'd expected. I had stepped into the big leagues with a peewee persona. I did not make it at McCreary long. But I was then sent to an even worse prison: Pollock, Louisiana, USP, aka "Gladiator School." This place had an endless supply of heroin, knives, meth, and alcohol.

I was soon using drugs again just to help me be the tough guy I felt I needed to be just to survive at this joint. I called my family and tricked them out of money, and made my girl do things neither of us wanted her doing. I was right back where I'd started. I was sick.

I signed up for the Challenge Program, a residential therapeutic community to help inmates adjust to prison life and to change their thinking errors. When administration called my name to move over to this program unit, the other guys protested, warning me that whites did not participate in "check-in" programs. I stood my ground and politicked my way into the program.

Then I made a fatal mistake.

The very first day, when asked to tell the Challenge community -- other inmates-- why I had joined, I made this statement on the microphone: "I moved over here to get off drugs."

Other inmates, especially the gang members, considered this telling --snitching-- they said it insinuated that there were drugs in the unit I'd moved from. The next day, on my way back from chow, two inmates jumped me. I slipped on the grass trying to escape their violence. As they kicked me repeatedly in the head, I remembered the people who had been killed at this prison and others who had been beaten into comas. I thought of my legacy and all the people I'd ripped off. All the people I had let down. I could not think of one single accomplishment. My life was flashing before my eyes, and all I was, was a combination of bad choices.

It seemed like forever before the officer got there to save me. I was escorted to SHU (Special Housing Unit) and put in an overcrowded cell. I had to lay my mat on the floor. I had two cellies and we were locked down together twenty-three hours a day. It was one of the worst experiences of my life. I was in pain, having been beaten black and blue, missing patches of hair, had cauliflower ears, and was also detoxing from heroin. I vowed yet again to never use drugs anymore.

The staff had a little pity on me and requested I be sent to a safer prison. I was sent to Tucson, Arizona. This place was sweet compared to Louisiana. It had zero politics. I could do anything I wanted - program, walk to chow by myself, get an education, party - whatever. I stayed sober for a couple of months. Then I convinced myself I could earn some extra money. I could hustle and show Lauren that I could take care of her even from the pen. I could send her money to come see me too.

Suddenly, my case manager called me into the office and told me to choose an F.C.I. (Federal Correctional Institution) close to home, that I was being transferred to an R-DAP facility. (Residential Drug Abuse Program). I could not believe my luck. Just a few months before, I had been in the most violent joint in America and now I was going to an F.C.I. Another chance to start fresh, get it right.

When I arrived at F.C.I. Petersburg Medium in Virginia, I learned that my cellies were both sex offenders. Violent gangs do not allow sex offenders to live around them. That told me the yard would be safe. I called my girl and asked her how much it would cost for her to come see me. She said eight hundred for a comfortable trip. I took advantage of the lower security at this prison, and started smuggling and selling drugs on the yard. I sent her nine hundred dollars, filled my locker up with commissary then ended up in the SHU on the very same day Lauren arrived.

I had not even made it a month and that was no one's fault but my own. I was too sober to blame my bad choices on drugs. I was forced to have an honest look at ME. This hurt so bad that I broke down.

All alone for the first time since sentencing I thought about how far I had gotten off course since the day I cried in that courtroom. I cried and cried, but I knew from experience that this wouldn't empower me to make good decisions. I had already been in this position on several occasions.

I could not blame drugs, the system, or individuals for the fool I saw in the mirror. To take an honest look at myself hurt. I dealt with the pain by ignoring the truth. I would escape reality with various distractions. Finally I found a distraction that was the answer to the fool in the mirror.

> A man who
> knows he is a fool
> is not a great fool.
>
> Chung-tzu

Your Transformation Story
Who have you become?

In this section, explore the events in your life that have taken you to a place you don't want to be. Honestly think about decisions you have made and how the consequences of those decisions affected your life. Here are some questions to get you started.

> ➢ Can you see yourself in Dustin's or Lonzo's story?
>
> ➢ Are you in character? Do you see a pattern to your life?
>
> ➢ Is your life's pattern working for you or against you?
>
> ➢ How would you describe your life at this point?
>
> ➢ Have you had enough?

Write it down.

Part III

HELP

Chapter 5
Help Comes From
the Strangest Places
Lonzo

Fool.

Fool was walking my way as I was questioning myself. Right on time. Fool was a high ranking member of the GDs. He was a gangsta for real and I had a lot of love and respect for him. He was exactly as his name. He was a fool. He exposed anybody that was faking. You had to be a real gangsta to even be around this dude. If you weren't sure of who you were or even serious about that lifestyle, you would feel uncomfortable when he came around. This dude was like that. The warden would come get him when we was locked down for serious issues and let him walk the joint, unit to unit, to squash whatever problem that was in the air so there wouldn't be any more bloodshed. Fool was good at keeping the peace too, but when it was time to go off, he was always ready. He'd been down since the early nineties. He's one of the old man's co-defendants, and one thing for sure, he loves the old man.

So as I was questioning myself, I saw him come up the stairs to holla at me. In my head, I'm like "Damn!" He was like "What's up, Breed?" That's what they used to call me, short for the organization I was in.

He began to start telling me, "Man, Joe, you on the right track, you doing something a lot of us don't have the courage to do. And I be messing with you 'cause I don't know what else to say. I don't know how to encourage someone to do the right thing because this is all I know. This is my life here. I got a couple life sentences. I may die in here, so doing what I do gives me a purpose to get up out that lil bunk in the mornings. I can't just give up my position and everything I worked hard for, because that would take me back to square one, a nobody and I can't spend the rest of my life in here like that. But you, you got a second chance out there on the street. You doing the right thing because you can't take this jail stuff out there on them streets. I'm proud of you man. Continue studying whatever it is you're studying. I see a big change in you. You the real soldier. It's rare to see a real dude, especially in this lifestyle, make that change and know that you ain't missing nothing. Oh, but I did hit them for three hundred dollars at the poker table last night! It's been sweet since you ain't been down there. I'm 'bout to go down there now, matter of fact. I'ma holler at you later, and know that the guys going to always have your back. 'Love G.'"

That conversation, right there, "that day" changed my life forever.

Fool's words were like confirmation from all the "real dudes" of that world that I was doing the right thing. That was exactly the encouragement I needed at that moment. A sense of belonging was what had been missing, and now I knew where I belonged.

That was a critical time for me and Allah knew it. He sent the perfect person at the perfect time! That was something like a miracle. Fool was not himself when he was talking to me. A more authoritative voice was speaking through him. It didn't even seem like we had just had that conversation at all, because when I looked down on the bottom tier, Fool had one of our homies, "Trouble," in a headlock because he was sitting in his chair at the poker table. I smiled and began to thank Allah for what He had just done for me.

"He will send help from the strangest places."

Lonzo's Explanation

AL-HAMDU LILAH (PRAISE GOD)

Chapter 6
Help me!
Dustin

In the SHU by myself I started thinking about all the hell I'd been through. Then it hit me -- most of it was my own fault. This truth hurt and hurt bad. I was hurting inside, but deep down I knew that tears would not help in the long run. I had put on my best thinking cap; I had had chance after chance to pursue my goals, but somehow, my best thinking had me always ending up right here.

WHY? WHY? WHY? I started to ask God out loud: WHY?

What I was really saying was "Help me, God. I have tried everything I can think of, but I always end up here. I need you to help me, God."

I waited, but He did not appear out of nowhere and I did not hear any loud voice and the more I thought about my situation, the worse I felt. I turned on my radio, trying to escape reality and to my surprise, God sounded through the speakers!

He started talking about the fall of Adam and my inherited nature and the rise of His Son Jesus Christ. My epiphany came with the realization that when I go through something tough for me, I blame someone else. Now I was hearing that I could blame my inherited nature, from Adam, and I was simultaneously provided the way out -- Jesus.

It was a moment I will never forget as long as I live, and according to God, that is eternity! I died to the flesh that day and was born of the Spirit. I inherited a new nature -- the nature of Christ.

I surrendered my life to Christ. I started writing letters to my family. I quoted scriptures like Galatians 2:20: "I have been crucified with Christ. It is no longer I who lives, but Christ who lives in me." In my letters, I expressed my surprising desire to stay in SHU. I was everything in God, but nothing in myself. I was fearful that the distractions of other people, along with the peer pressure to use drugs, would corrupt my relationship with God. My mother, though, called my counselor crying, saying "I think my son has been through too much. He is losing his mind."

She was wrong; I had already lost it.

Christ was restoring me to sanity.

When I was released back into general population, I was scared to death. Scriptures like "I'm a new creature in Christ" were very appealing to me. I was trying really hard to consider myself a brand new man. I did not want to do anything that would indicate otherwise. I was protective of my testimony. I had been one person on the compound before this conversion; now I was different. What could I expect from my former friends?

I had to use my Bible to make everyday choices. I did not want to get it wrong. I did succumb to a bit of social pressure from some old friends and started working out with them again. I explained my newfound beliefs and most of them started going to church with me. We all agreed not to cuss and if someone slipped, we would do twenty-five push-ups together.

I invited a Christian brother I met in church to work out with us. When the guys found out he was a sex offender, they came to me complaining. I had read in my Bible:

"You would rather tie a millstone around your neck than offend one of God's children."

I quoted this scripture to the two guys pushing the issue. They said they were going to confront the sex offender and ask him about his charge. I explained how that would be offensive to him, that he was a new creation in Christ. They insisted so I let them know I wanted nothing to do with it.

In less than two weeks the main aggressor of that situation ended up in SHU. He went crazy, tore his toilet off the wall, popped the sprinkler in his cell, and hit the door for ten hours straight. Administration did a special transfer to get him out of this institution. I told myself he would rather have a millstone tied around his neck than to be in the position he was in. Within a couple more weeks, the other guy quit working out completely and a bunch of sores started to surface on his face and arms. This seemed to me verification of both of what my trials as a new Christian would be and that I would be delivered of them if I held fast and let God Himself handle the retribution.

I enrolled in Nations University, pursuing a degree in Religious Studies. I'd completed my GED in lockup; now a college degree was on the horizon.

The elder of our church here, Donnie Howell, moved me in the cell with him. He was instrumental to my transformation and I hold him in high esteem. I respect him so much. He has a life sentence. He's been in the same cell for seven years. And he never misses church. He was and is an example for me. He showed me that the Lord will keep me. That what I was going through was more than a phase. I believe God sent Donnie to help me. He is a great man of God and I can't overestimate his positive influence on me. He took me under his wing and treated me like his son.

He called me up one Sunday to read a scripture in front of the congregation. I turned blood red. My mouth was so dry I couldn't speak. I was that nervous. I got embarrassed to the point I wanted to run out of the church.

That night when we locked down, I started reading the Bible aloud. Every night I would read for hours that way. Donnie would usually fall right to sleep but I would keep reading. Then he would get up every morning around 4:00 a.m. and pray, read, and meditate on the scripture.

Christ had freed me from drug addiction and the only thing hanging on from my old lifestyle was my girl and some false beliefs.

Lauren started making comments like "I don't even know you anymore." I would call her all happy. I would share a testimony with her about what God had done or was going to do in our lives and she would blow it off as a small coincidence or false hope. I

60

thought she was simply sad, or convicted because she was not able to get sober herself. She seemed less and less happy as I felt more and more free. I prayed: "God, if she is not the one I can do your will with, have her leave me. I can't make it happen, God."

I felt like I was climbing the ladder without her. I did not want to leave her behind, but if she wasn't willing to climb, I needed her to let me go.

I violated a Bureau of Prison rule on Christmas by making a three-way phone call to her. On January fourth, I was in my cell reading the Bible when I received an incident report for violation of code 297, "Abuse of telephone privileges." This upset me. Christians are not supposed to get in trouble. Later I got on the computer and I had an E-mail waiting. My girl had written "I'm sorry I didn't tell you sooner but I moved in with someone December fourth."

I sent her this song: "So Long, Goodbye," by 10 Years and deleted her from my e-mail account. I then wrote my mother this e-mail:

"Mom I got a write-up for calling Lauren and it crushed me. I'm fighting as hard as I can to stand my post with the Lord. I know this is a test of my faith and I'm trying not to stress so I can see a victorious solution. I was only trying to hold us together. I wanted to help her fight her addiction. And she was living with another man the whole time. I'm not even her man and I was convinced I was doing the right thing."

It was another trial for me and I held on to my faith that God would see me through.

About two weeks later, I moved to a different unit so I could be in R-DAP, the Residential Drug Abuse Program. It's a behavior modification program that allows inmates to govern each other. We have professionals who facilitate groups and keep track of our progress, but for the most part we help each other. I was saved, and I had been sober for about six months. I was amazed how everyone in this new unit saw me. They acted like I was some saint. My peers made positive comments and would use me as a model of good behavior. Maybe I was a new creation.

Then I met a white-collar criminal, educated and with a fortunate upbringing. He began to discredit my intelligence and insights. He would say things like "You're a parrot, all you do is repeat what you've read," and "You're not smart, there's a gap so big between who you are and who you think you are that a Mack truck could drive through it."

I responded by telling him I would beat him up. I immediately felt bad for saying those words and I knew I had validated everything he'd just said by my overreaction.

I started to go into a little bit of a depression. I secluded myself in my cell. One day I was lying there thinking of how everyone had seen me react negatively to the comments Mr. Brilliant had made, when Mr. Stanley, a black Muslim from Chicago, come in my cell. He told me: "I love you brother. Get up out dat bed. We got work to do."

As I walked out of the cell, another guy who is always getting in trouble told me, "I got you figured out."

I smiled, but dreaded what was coming next. I said, "Oh yeah?"

He said, "Yeah, you're a gangsta for God."

I responded defensively, "Yeah, you're right. My shot caller is O.G. Jesus. Omnipresent God. Omnipotent God. Omniscient God. He sees everything and never sends me on a dummy mission. He knows the heart of man." We both laughed and walked our separate ways.

A couple of months later, I lost my temper again and my friend, Mr. Stanley, told me he thought I would beat someone up if they said something disparaging about my faith. This was both a compliment and constructive criticism. I was proud of my Lord and Savior, but somehow reluctant to lose some of my old attitudes. These "trials" kept bringing them back up.

The next time someone offended me, I was determined not to sin. When Mr. Brilliant made one of his comments to me, it provoked the same anger and desire for revenge within me. I had to try really hard to not respond inappropriately. I ran to my cell and began writing. I channeled my emotions into my first newsletter article:

Freedom is Yours
R.D.A.P.
Mr. Lonzo Stanley

By: Dustin Frisbee

A career offender serving two hundred months for distribution of cocaine goes from a high ranking member of a notorious Chicago street gang to a religious square in hopes of becoming the man he was created to be.

Exposing himself to a harsh environment, stripping layer upon layer of criminal flaws, he sacrificed all perceived benefits while dealing with both his inner self and the way people experienced his transition. There are no words to give his inner struggle justice, but we all know how uncomfortable change is, even in a therapeutic community. It can all be summed up in one word:

COURAGE.

Let's give credit where credit is due. We are talking about a man who left everything to be nobody in hopes of being somebody. A man who lived for instant gratification for twenty years gave up everything he had for a life that is still years away.

Continued

Freedom is Yours *continued*

When I asked him about his inner struggle, status, future, and jailhouse respect, he said, "The hardest thing I ever had to do was the best thing I ever did." Mr. Stanley set aside everything the criminal lifestyle had taught him, and tolerated the humiliation of being wrong in hopes of being right. He embraced the pain of change so he can learn a new way. Many times, he has second guessed himself and wondered if his transformation is worth it. Instead of giving up, he increases his odds by choosing to fill in the gap.

Mr. Stanley's change in thinking, belief, expectation, and attitude covered many miles, taking him from an illiterate gang-banger to the humble reader (and leader) he is today. He started last in his G.E.D. class, not knowing how to read, and finished first. This community voted him Peer of the Month, because he is a well-respected man of integrity.

All Mr. Stanley wants to do is be "RIGHT" and know what he can do to help others. It is his hope that his story of transformation will inspire you to take a similar path.

> "It takes courage to grow up and become who you really are."
> E. E. Cummings

This was a moment for both me and Mr. Stanley. For me, it meant I could control my feelings in a positive way.

But I had started justifying my anger with scripture like "Be angry and sin not." I knew deep down something was not right about the way I was so easily rattled, but I tried to convince myself that it was normal by emphasizing "be angry." Now I was stooping to using scripture to manipulate.

The next time someone said something to arouse those negative feelings, I said, "You're lucky I'm not the old me." When I calmed down, I thought "how stupid was that?" so I prayed, "God, heal me! Help me get control over myself, so I can be of greater use to you. I need you, God. I'm asking you to help me"

The next week we graduated R_DAP and, ironically, Mr. Brilliant and Lonzo Stanley each gave speeches. God spoke to me that day. Mr. Stanley explained to us how he got to the point where he is now in his life. He stated that he had to trace himself back to his childhood to find the little boy he left behind.

Dustin's Explanation

I have a strong desire to be right. It was very hard for me to accept help. I had to put my pride aside daily and receive what I needed to receive. It takes courage to break the cycle and it's only broken with help. My biggest weakness was acting as if I had all the answers. Humility has helped me be a better man.

> Everyone needs help from everyone.
>
> Bertolt Brecht

Your Transformation Story
Where is your help?

Do you need help? Let this book help you. Let go of whatever is holding you back. Step out of your comfort zone and do what we did in these next few chapters - transform.

Here are some questions to help you:

> ➤ What aspects of Dustin's and Lonzo's stories could you identify with?
>
> ➤ Are you always blaming someone else?
>
> ➤ Who do you look up to? Do these people have your best interests in mind?
>
> ➤ Are you AWARE of the decisions you make and the consequences of them?
>
> ➤ Do you believe in a higher power?
>
> ➤ Do you have the courage to change?

Write it down.

This may be an especially hard section to write. Don't worry if it doesn't make sense at first. Put your thoughts on paper. Write down any troubling incidents you are involved in. Put the writing away for a couple of days. Come back and read what you have written. Has your perspective changed? Keep doing this until you notice a pattern. Could you have handled things differently? Write about what you could have done.

When the student is
ready, the teacher
will appear.

Ancient proverb

Part IV

TRANSFORMATION

Chapter 7
I Found Myself
Lonzo

By me staying out of the way in Terre Haute, I finally got the chance to transfer to an FCI, a medium security, in Greenville, Illinois. This was going to be a totally different experience for me because in every joint I had ever walked into, I had an identity. I always went in introducing myself as Lonzo, a New Breed Black Gangsta from the west side of Chicago. But this time I went in as a Nobody. I told the guys back at Terre Haute that when I left that spot I was going to put the game and that lifestyle behind me. They heard me, but I knew how things worked in a maximum security prison. That's why I said, "When I *leave* this spot," because in joints like that one, the only way you're going to get out of something you sign up for is in a bag or on a stretcher.

Early 2011. I will never forget the day I stepped on the compound of FCI Greenville, Illinois. Three guys were waiting on me at the door of R and D. They were New Breeds. They had gotten word I was on my way there and had big bags of stuff for me. I knew one of the guys, MJ, from another spot. I gave MJ a hug and a smile and told him that I appreciated the bags and stuff but that I was no longer a New Breed.

The look on his face was of disappointment and a sense of disbelief. The other guys had that same look and they didn't even know me. MJ started to explain how this joint was different from the pen and that it didn't have all the militant rules of a pen and so on. I stopped him and let him know that it wasn't about all that. This was something I chose and had to do for me and my salvation. Disappointed, and out of love for me, he reached in one of the bags and gave me some items that would hold me over until I got my property. I asked him where 2-B Unit was and headed that way.

The first day I went out to the yard was one of my hardest days. I felt out of place, alone, and lost. This was my first time hitting a yard and I didn't have a spot to go chop it up with the guys. Every gang and organization had their own section of the yard and I had always had mine where I fit in. But not today. I was lost. I didn't know what to do so I just walked the track by myself.

I saw guys looking and pointing and I knew what that was about. I also knew that this was something I had to go through to get where I needed to be in life. I can't lie, this was hard for me because I felt like I was losing myself and my identity. But as I gradually got comfortable being on my own and standing on my own two feet, I started to learn things about myself that I never knew.

I started to like and even love my own company! I started challenging myself, like stopping use of the N-word. I started setting short term goals for myself. And what I thought was hard became easier and easier for me.

Leaving the organization was the hardest thing I ever had to do, but it was actually the best thing I ever did. I began talking and communicating with people I never would have associated with. Talking with them helped open up a new world to me.

I got to studying and reading things that were very interesting and were challenging my old beliefs. In doing that, I also began to shake off the old ways of thinking that had led me to where I was now. My thoughts and my heart were being shaped the way they were created to operate: right. I learned to detach myself from my past experiences so that I couldn't keep living in the past and making decisions on certain things that happened to me long ago. I had to learn how to live and make decisions in the present moment. In doing that, we can make the best decisions we need to make to take us to that next level in life.

Making our own decisions and doing something for ourselves is one of the best things we can do. If we're not doing something for ourselves behind these walls or even out in the free world, we're at a standstill and are setting ourselves up for failure. We have to have a plan, I told myself. We have to have some goals and they have to be on paper. We can't say we are going to do something and not have it down on paper. That would be like travelling in a strange city without a map or GPS.

It doesn't have to be a big plan and the goals don't have to be big either. What helped me most was making plans for the outside world. Simple plans and goals helped me prepare more for my release. Just planning for the outside world frees a person's mind and keeps it away from getting caught up in jail thinking.

You can start off with some small goals like I did, such as:

- ✓ Find a job within three weeks.
- ✓ Pay a close family member or close friend to stay with them just until I get on my feet.
- ✓ Within six weeks save $1200 to buy a car to get around.
- ✓ In six more weeks, save another $1200 to get an apartment.

Those were my goals when I first started to write my plans out and every couple of months my plans and goals would get bigger and bigger. Just writing the plan out does something for your life and your spirit. It gives you the drive to want more out of your life. You have to have a plan. It is a must.

We have to change: we can't continue to think like criminals. We're not criminals; we are men, good men that could do great things. Our children, mothers, wives, siblings, and community need us. They need men, real men.

If we don't change now, the world will never get any better. It will continue to get worse and just imagine how the world, our kids and grandkids would look when they're living in it twenty years from now. NOW is the time for us to do our part and our part is to take the necessary steps so we can help change this crazy world.

If you look at it this way, you see: "Change you, you change a whole generation."

I will not lie, change is not easy. But I'm here to tell you that it is possible.

Let's do it. We can do it together.

Lonzo's Explanation

When I first got to Greenville, I didn't know what I was going to do. I just knew that I wanted something different in my life.

People say that they don't care what people think about them. For me, I can't lie, I cared what people thought about me and that slowed down my process of doing what I was supposed to be doing in life that would have taken me to the next level.

I had to always remind myself that what I was doing was for me and my loved ones. I used to be apprehensive about trying new things that would give me identity. I had to tell myself that I don't know these people in here and they don't know me, so why not practice and experiment with them to become the true me? The first thing I did was cut the braids off my head. I had to get my grown man look on. Then I started saying good morning to certain people. It didn't feel normal at first because I wasn't used to greeting people like that.

Then I started to switch up my appearance by pulling up my pants to my waistline and wearing shirts that actually fit me. I tried all kinds of different things until I found me.

People thought I was burned out (crazy), but I didn't care because I was on a mission to find Lonzo J. Stanley.

Hopefully after reading this, you can start your own mission to find YOURSELF.

Chapter 8
Thank You, I'm Very Grateful
Dustin

I knew that tracing myself back was going to be hard for me. First, I had to get past the lie that I was okay, that I had it all together. If I was really going to be a new creation, I had to get rid of whatever negativity and unforgiveness that I was hanging on to from my childhood. I rushed Mr. Stanley after his speech and we agreed to help each other.

He would help me trace myself back if I would help him write his story. I was more excited about writing than I was about tracing myself back. In fact, I started writing immediately.

I would write all through count and run to Mr. Stanley's cell to read it to him as soon as the doors popped. Maybe he thought, like my old celly in county jail, that I was "buggin' out." But he would always smile and encourage me before he strategically started digging toward the root of my problems. When it was time to work my chapter, I hesitated. He came to my cell and started telling me how great I was, how good I was going to do and how much courage it took to face the truth. He told me there was nothing to be ashamed of. I knew I had to free myself from the false belief that drove away everyone who could help me and prevented God from using me in the way He desired. My personal false belief was that I was not good enough, that I was "less than."

The morning I first lost myself, I was standing in that line at school all those years ago, comparing myself to Ben. I was asking myself questions like, "Why don't I have my father's last name?" and making mental notes, such as: even if I did have an L.L. Bean backpack, "Frisbee," Mom's weird last name, would be stitched on it. I was considering myself unworthy of such when the teacher pulled me aside and sent me to the principal's office for dress code failure.

This remembrance helped me answer the questions I was asking myself. The shame or embarrassment I felt confirmed my perceptions.

I had been in that office feeling "less than." I was sitting as low as I could in my chair, trying not to exist, when my angry mother bolted through the door. She was mad at the school, and this made me feel loved. Her anger was contagious. I stopped thinking about me and became angry with the preps, the students who were more financially fortunate. This helped me cope with the hurt I felt from the false beliefs I was developing.

I told myself I was okay. I told my mother I was okay. When I went to a new school, I tried to appear okay. But I was still hanging onto the lie I had internalized that day.

I had a deep fear of rejection, so I pretended I knew everything. If someone challenged this, I would completely shut down on them or drive them away with aggressive behavior. The thought that I was unworthy or "less than" protected its space in my brain by manifesting itself as negative feelings that caused me to misbehave. Then that would cover itself with another lie. The lie that I was okay, that I did not need help. The lie that it was anyone else's fault but mine.

In the beginning I could believe my problems were someone else's fault, but after many repetitive screw-ups, blaming someone else was no longer sufficient in my mind. By this time I was acknowledging my addictions, blaming my behavior on it. I would tell myself and others it was not me. I had only done whatever because of the drugs.

When Christ freed me from addictions I could not use this lie anymore. I did not want to use it. As a matter of fact, I didn't even know it was a lie until my problems didn't go away with my addiction. The lie that I was a failure could not be very easily dismissed.

When I started to absolutely refuse to be a criminal, I learned to make a distinction between my good and bad thoughts. I connected my bad thoughts to evil and this helped me eradicate who I was as a felon. II Corinthians 10:4-5:

For the weapons of our warfare are not carnal but mighty through God to the pulling down of strongholds;

Casting down imaginations, and every high thing that exalteth itself against the things of God, and bringing into captivity every thought to the obedience of Christ.

showed me how I could be actively involved in pursuing the promise God made me in Jeremiah 29:11:

For I know the plans I have for you, declares the Lord,

Plans to prosper you and not to harm you, plans to give you hope and a future.

When opportunities came that allowed me to have a positive experience, I would ignore my feelings and cast down imaginations that were contradictory to the teachings of Christ.

To turn the other cheek, or walk away from high risk situations is not very rewarding in prison, but instead of praying for God to take away my trials, I learned in Romans 5:1-5 to look forward to them, because that's how God shapes me into the man I want to be.

Romans 5:1-5: We have been made right with God because of our faith. Now we have a peace with Him because of our Lord Jesus Christ.

Through faith in Jesus we have received God's grace.

In that grace we stand. We are full of joy because we expect to share in God's glory.

And that's not all. We are full of joy even when we suffer. We know our suffering gives us the strength to go on. The strength to go on produces character. Character produces hope. And hope will never let us down.

God has poured His love in our hearts. He did it through the Holy Spirit, whom He has given us.

Not too long after I came to this understanding, my celly cussed me out for asking him to clean up after himself. He became really aggressive with me and I was able to control my reaction. I was not even angry. I had compassion for him. I let him vent and a couple of days later he came to me apologizing. He explained that he was going through some problems at home. He felt helpless and it made him angry. I explained that he was not helpless, that we could pray.

I was able to allow God to work through me in that moment with a genuine prayer for his family. He was open to this not because of his faith, but because my response during his rant had not turned him away. I prayed with all sincerity and when he rushed out of the cell so I wouldn't see his teary eyes, I hit my knees and starting thanking God for bringing me so far.

Since then I have become known as somewhat of a prayer warrior. People come to me and ask for prayer for their kids, parents, GED tests, and personal problems. This does as much for me as it does for them. It reassures me that I am worthy. That I have a purpose.

There's nothing like seeing a convict who acts tough on the yard open up and let you help him. I pray with confidence, speaking to the root of their problems. I speak with the authority of Christ, backed by the word of God. I tell these men who they really are in Christ without shame or regret. I encourage them to trace themselves back to find that little boy they lost and to give him a new purpose.

I was unaware of the erroneous beliefs that governed my behavior until I asked myself why I felt the way I felt in certain situations. What I discovered was that the majority of my boundaries were connected to false beliefs - misconceptions I had developed as a child. The feeling I was experiencing was connected to these "automatic thoughts" or devil's lies that surfaced at just the right time, causing me to react inappropriately, keeping me from receiving help, or from doing new productive things I wanted to do. By replacing these thoughts with appropriate truths, my comfort zone expanded. And I experienced more and more freedom to reveal the true ME.

> Man has the key to understanding and solving his psychological disturbances within the scope of his own awareness.
>
> Aaron Beck.

> Service to others is the rent you pay for your room here on earth.
>
> Muhammad Ali

Your Transformation Story
What has been transformed?

This section will be ongoing for the rest of your life. Once on the path, you will notice little things that are transformed every day, if you let them. Do something positive out of your comfort zone and write about what happened because of it.

Here are some things to think about:

➤ What are the lies in your lifestyle?

➤ Do you have the courage to stand alone in your convictions?

➤ Have you ever written down goals and tried to achieve them?

➤ Can you detach from your past experiences?

➤ Make a list of the important people in your life. What are the qualities and characteristics of these people that you admire?

➤ Make a list of the qualities and characteristics that you want to develop in yourself.

➤ Make a list of goals to achieve tomorrow. Next week. Next month. Next year.

➤ Make a list of things that have been transformed in your life. Keep adding to this list as time goes on.

Do what we did, start writing.

END NOTE

We share our stories with you because we want you to overcome every obstacle that stands in your way. Whether the obstacle is a mental roadblock or an adverse set of circumstances, if you are reading this right now, be encouraged. Let this inspire you into action. Do what your mind tells you that you do not deserve, and be what people said you couldn't be. Surround yourself with positive people and feed off their energy. If you are not motivated by this point, you need to get out of your own way and allow yourself to receive what you need to receive.

We look forward to hearing of your victory.

E-mail us at:

TransformationinBlackandWhite@gmail.com

Share your stories with us.

TRANSFORMATION BEGINS NOW!!!

Upcoming Publication

Man on a Mission

By Dustin Frisbee

I have found sobriety in Christ Jesus, and am now on my way to being a father to my beautiful daughter Madison and blessed son Lavery Allen. The upcoming book *Man on a Mission* will start that journey where this one left off, with me heading in the direction of fatherhood.

Be encouraged and begin your own journey.

Contact Dustin:

DustinFrisbee86@outlook.com

Dustin Frisbee 44895074
P.O. Box1000
Petersburg, Va 23804

Made in the USA
Middletown, DE
08 August 2016